Architecture in Pen and Ink

McGraw-Hill Books of Related Interest

BURDEN • *Entourage: A Tracing File for Architecture and Interior Design Drawing*

CROWE • *Architectural Rendering: An International Perspective*

KNOLL, HECHINGER • *Architectural Models: Construction Techniques*

KOPLAR • *Architectural Studies: A Step-by-Step Guide to Rendering and Drawing Techniques*

Architecture in Pen and Ink

John S. M. Chen, AIA

McGraw-Hill, Inc.

New York   San Francisco   Washington, D.C.   Auckland   Bogotá
Caracas   Lisbon   London   Madrid   Mexico City   Milan
Montreal   New Delhi   San Juan   Singapore
Sydney   Tokyo   Toronto

Library of Congress Cataloging-in-Publication Data

Architecture in pen and ink / [drawings compiled by] John S. M. Chen.
    p.   cm.
  ISBN 0-07-011079-4
    1. Architectural drawing—Catalogs.   2. Pen drawing—Catalogs.
  I. Chen, John S. M.
  NA2700.A67   1995
  720'.22'2—dc20   94-13895
                                                                          CIP

1 2 3 4 5 6 7 8 9 0   KP/KP   9 0 9 8 7 6 5 4

ISBN 0-07-011079-4

*The sponsoring editor for this book was Joel Stein, the
editing supervisor was Jane Palmieri, and the production
supervisor was Don Schmidt. It was set by McGraw-Hill's
Professional Book Group composition unit.*

Printed and bound by The Kingsport Press.

This book is printed on acid-free paper.

CONTENTS

INTRODUCTION

Pen and ink drawing is an important medium in architectural presentation. Unlike pencil or water-based media, pen and ink drawing is built up by the different density of black lines and dots, thus eliminating the less readable medium tones created by the softness or toned down washes of other media. In other words, every line and every dot in a pen and ink drawing are absolutely black and the paper which acts as a background is normally white, therefore creating the highest possible contrast. This makes the pen and ink drawing the most reproducible medium. It could be easily printed by a diazo machine, a camera, and even a copy machine can make perfect prints of it.

During the past, pen and ink drawings were usually drawn with the nib pen. The development of the fountain pen, especially the technical pen and markers, brought a new era to pen and ink drawings. The fountain pen is like the nib pen with an ink storage system. It is flexible and can draw lines with different widths to create drawings with strong personal character. It is usually used to draw study drawings or field sketches, such as the study drawings of Helmut Jahn and Stanley Tigerman and the field sketches by Frank Ching and others.

The most fascinating tool in the development of architectural pen and ink drawing is the technical pen that we now use everyday. The technical pen is called the *needle pen* in the Orient. This needle device enables the pen to draw continuous even lines. It was first used for construction drawings, but later people discovered it was also ideal for presentation drawings. Paul Rudolph uses this characteristic of the technical pen to draw presentation drawings strictly composed of straight lines, which can hardly be achieved by the nib pen. Using stippling to stimulate the texture of the subject is one of the advantages of the technical pen as done in drawings by Rael D. Slutsky and Manuel Avila. The tubular nib of the technical pen holds ink more efficiently than the nib pen and can produce numerous dots in a fraction of time. The other advantage of the technical pen is that its tubular nib can glide in any direction over the paper, but the nib pen cannot strike against the grain of the paper. This enables the illustrator to draw freehand presentation drawings or other drawings with a personal touch.

Markers, especially the fineline markers or felt pens are excellent tools for freehand sketching. They have the flexibility of the nib pen, which can draw lines with different widths and can move in any direction, regardless of the grain of the paper. This flexibility of the fineline marker can be seen in the study drawings of Peter Eisenman and the field sketches of the author.

Applying colors to pen and ink drawings is a more recent tendency in the development of pen and ink drawings. Pen and ink drawings can be integrated with color pencils, markers, or watercolors. About 10 years ago, Helmut Jahn began to apply color ink and pencils to his pen and ink study drawings in order to further enhance his ideas. Some illustrators often have a black and white and a color version of the same work. Among these illustrators are Rael D. Slutsky, Gene Streett, Manual Avila, Howard Associates, and others. Mr. Streett applies color markers to his drawings; Mr. Slutsky and Mr. Avila apply color pencils to their drawings; and, Howard Associates use watercolors. These colored pen and ink drawings are not included in this book, but they will be included in another book which is in the process of being assembled.

The technical pen, the fineline marker, and the fountain pen have changed the style of architectural pen and ink drawings. Today, there are many unique styles of architectural pen and ink drawing with each having its own distinct character. This book is a portfolio of these different architectural pen and ink drawings. It could be used as a learning file or a reference book.

Pen and ink drawings are becoming more and more popular among architects, landscape architects, interior designers, and illustrators. It is one of the best-loved mediums in architectural presentation.

ACKNOWLEDGMENTS

This architectural pen and ink book is made possible by many architects, illustrators, and other individuals who contributed their work. Special thanks to foreign contributors from Canada, China, Sweden, and other countries.

I am very grateful to Daniel Herbert and Steve Oles, who gave me early advice and direction which made all the difference in the progression of this book. Helmut Jahn and Frank Ching are the two early contributors, without their initiative I could not have compiled so many drawings from those known in the field. I would also like to thank those architects and their staff members that I have interviewed at the offices of Paul Rudolph, Helmut Jahn, Stanley Tigerman, and Cesar Pelli.

At a difficult time during the project I received special help from Harry Robinson, III, Dean of the School of Architecture and Planning at Howard University. I am also grateful to Kathryn Prigmore, Associate Dean; Victor Dzidzienyo, Departmental Chairman; Prof. Asghar Minai, Prof. Ken Jadin, and the rest of the faculty with whom I discussed my ideas and gained their support for the project.

I would like to express special appreciation to Ms. Renee Ford and Ms. Lesli Franklin for their help in editing and typing.

My gratitude extends to my wife, Hui Fang. Without her everyday encouragement and patience, this book could not be a reality, and I dedicate this book to her.

STUDY DRAWINGS
IN PEN AND INK

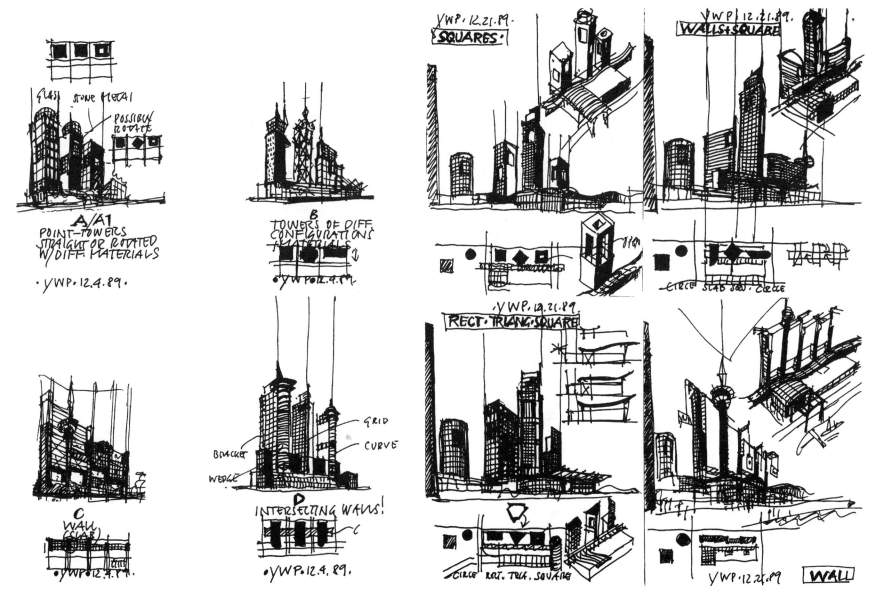

HELMUT JAHN: Study drawing for Yokohama Harbor, Japan. *Mont Blanc fountain pen on bond paper.* [*Courtesy Murphy/Jahn Inc. Architects.*]

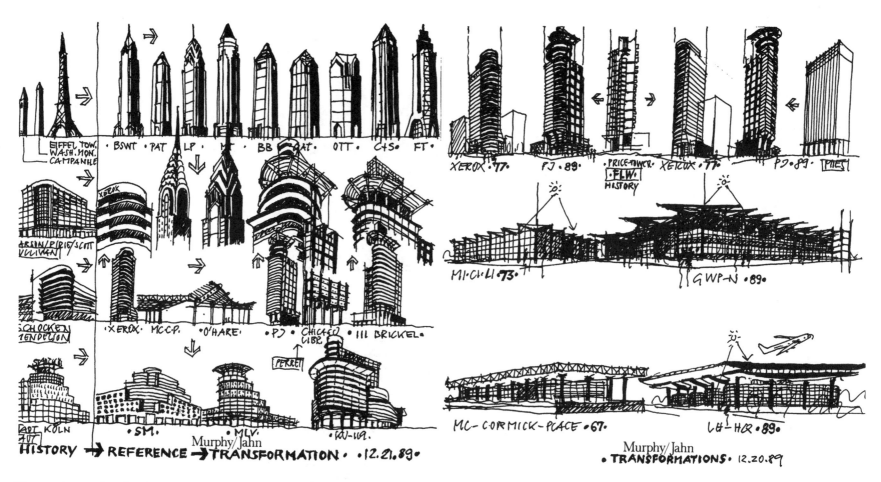

HELMUT JAHN: Study drawing for History/Reference/Transformation. *Porsche fountain pen on bond paper.*
[*Courtesy Murphy/Jahn Inc. Architects.*]

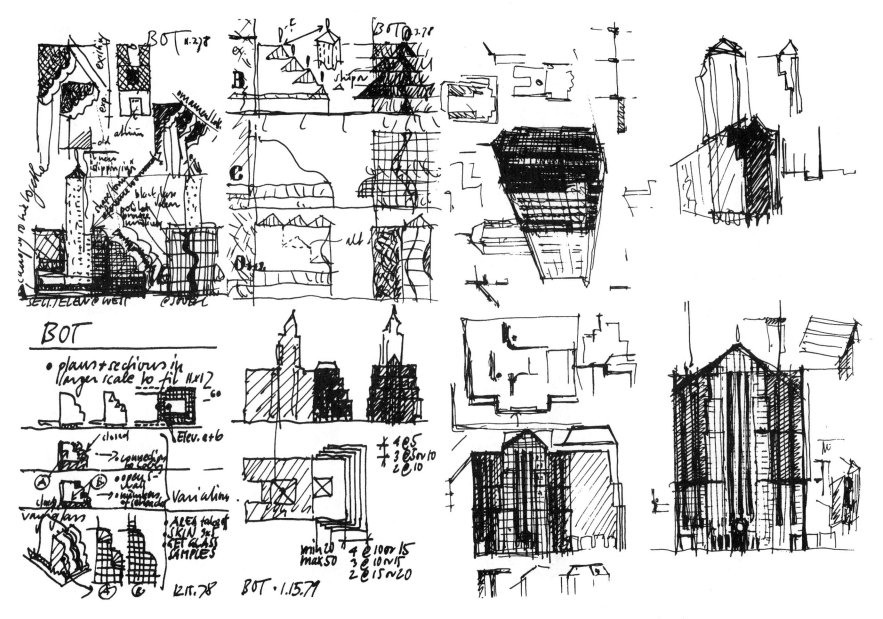

HELMUT JAHN: Study drawing for Board of Trade Addition, Chicago, Illinois. *Mont Blanc fountain pen on bond paper.*
[*Courtesy Murphy/Jahn Inc. Architects.*]

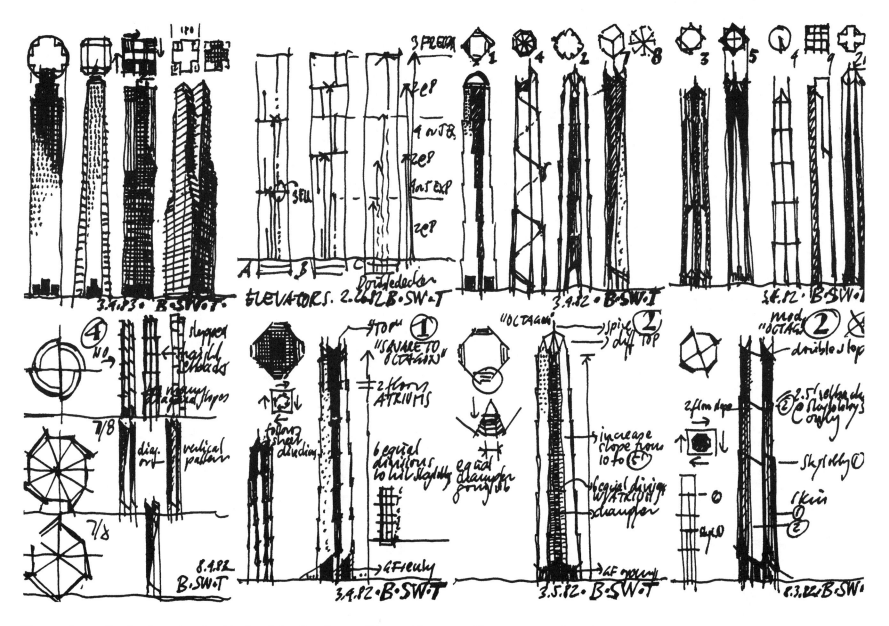

HELMUT JAHN: Study drawing for Bank of the Southwest Tower, Houston, Texas. *Mont Blanc fountain pen on bond paper.*
[*Courtesy Murphy/Jahn Inc. Architects.*]

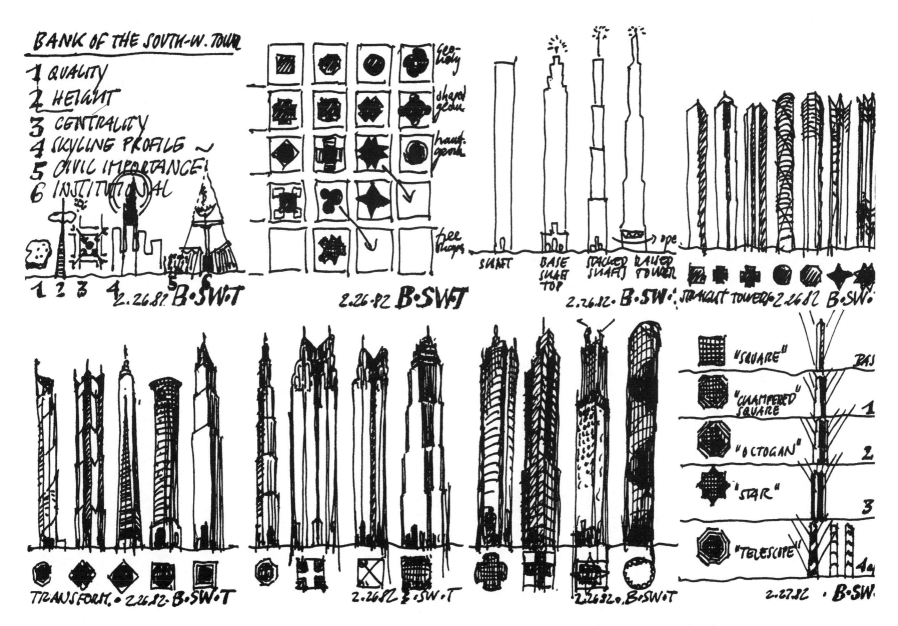

HELMUT JAHN: Study drawing for Bank of the Southwest Tower, Houston, Texas. *Mont Blanc fountain pen on bond paper.*
[*Courtesy Murphy/Jahn Inc. Architects.*]

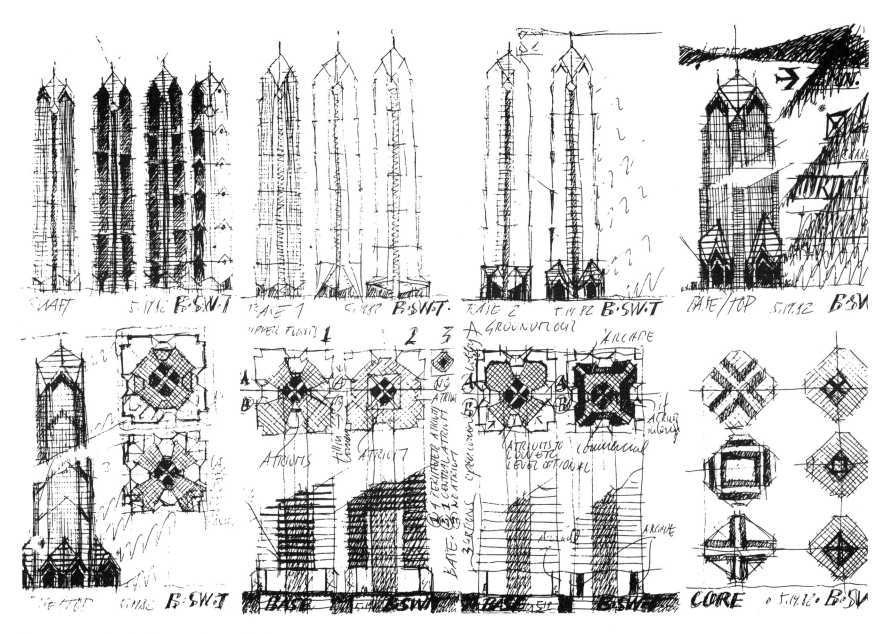

HELMUT JAHN: Study drawing for Bank of the Southwest Tower, Houston, Texas. *Mont Blanc fountain pen on bond paper.* [*Courtesy Murphy/Jahn Inc. Architects.*]

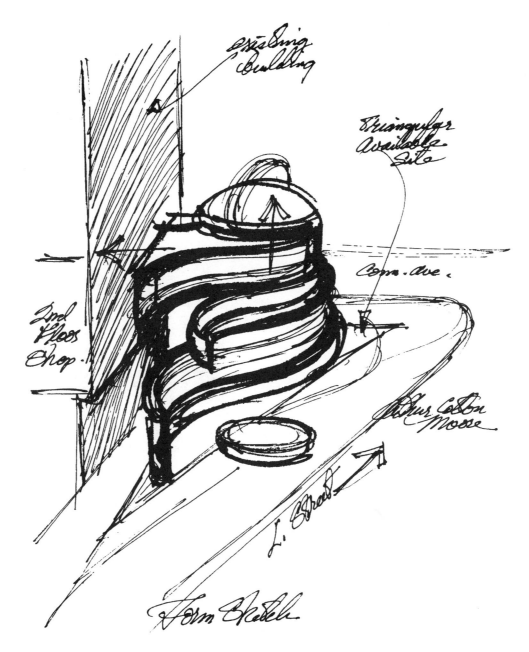

existing building

Triangular Available Site

Conn. Ave.

2nd Floor Shop.

Arthur Cotton Moore

L. Street

Form Sketch

ARTHUR COTTON MOORE: Study drawing for Rizik Pavilion at 1100 Connecticut Ave., Washington, D.C. *Marker, Pentel rolling writer pen on newsprint paper.* [*Courtesy Arthur Cotton Moore.*]

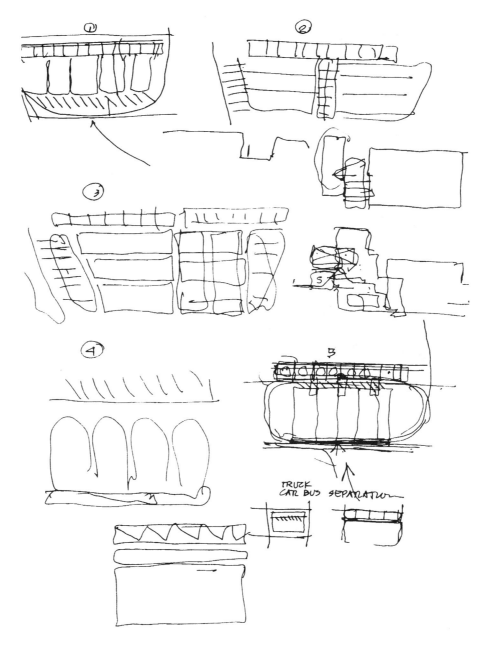

PETER EISENMAN: Study sketch for Columbus Convention Center, Columbus, Ohio. *Black felt pen on yellow tracing paper.*
[*Courtesy Eisenman Architects.*]

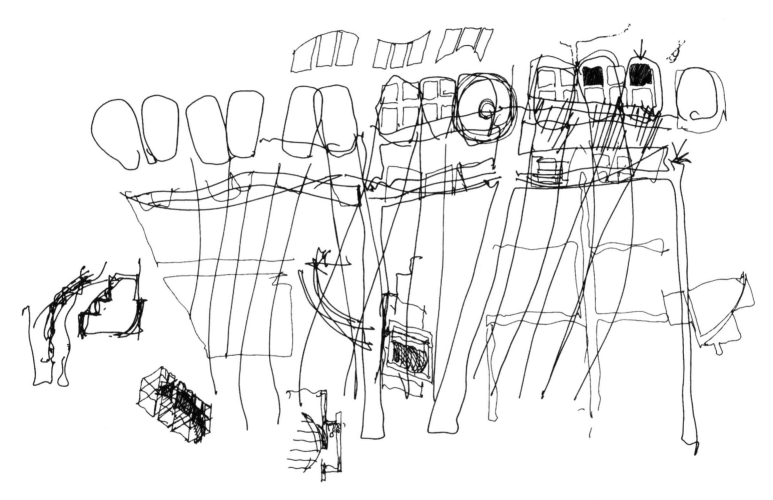

PETER EISENMAN: **Study sketch for Columbus Convention Center, Columbus, Ohio.** *Black felt pen on yellow tracing paper.* [*Courtesy Eisenman Architects.*]

PETER EISENMAN: Study sketch for DAAP, University of Cincinnati, Cincinnati, Ohio. *Black felt pen on vellum.*
[*Courtesy Eisenman Architects.*]

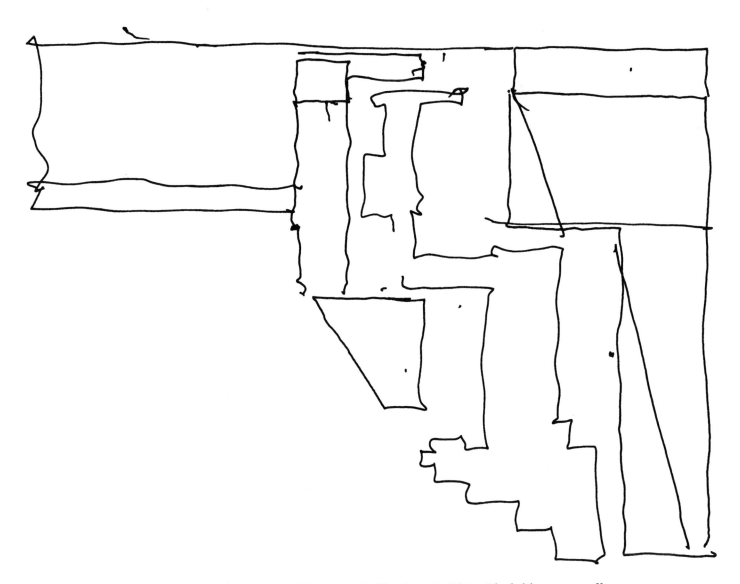

PETER EISENMAN: Study sketch for DAAP, University of Cincinnati, Cincinnati, Ohio. *Black felt pen on vellum.*
[*Courtesy Eisenman Architects.*]

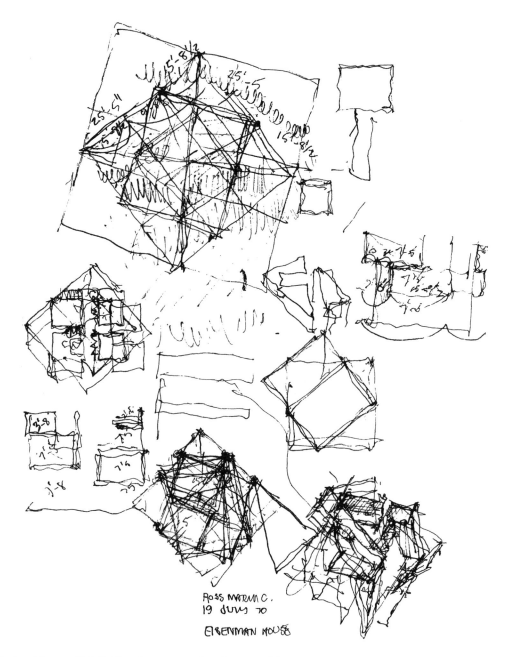

PETER EISENMAN: Study sketch for House IV. *Ball point pen on bond paper.* [*Courtesy Eisenman Architects.*]

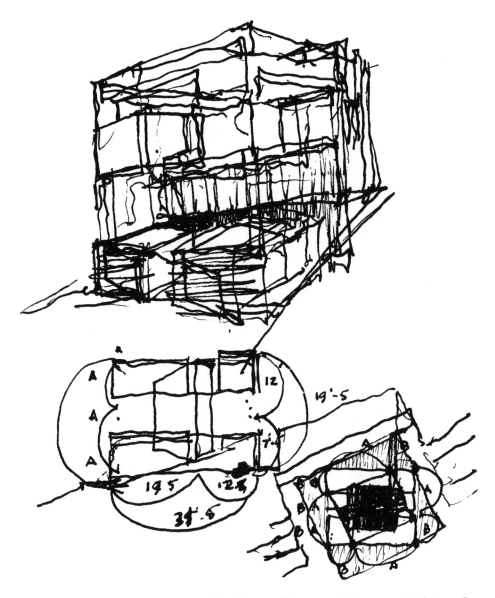

PETER EISENMAN: Study sketch for House IV. *Ball point pen on bond paper. [Courtesy Eisenman Architects.]*

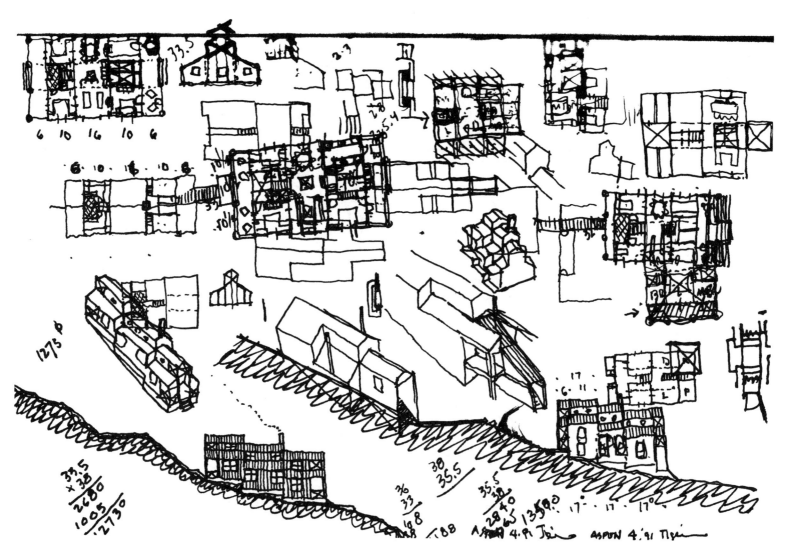

STANLEY TIGERMAN: Study drawing for Tigerman Weekend House, Aspen, Colorado (not built). *Mont Blanc fountain pen on acid-free paper.*
[*Courtesy Tigerman McCurry Architects.*]

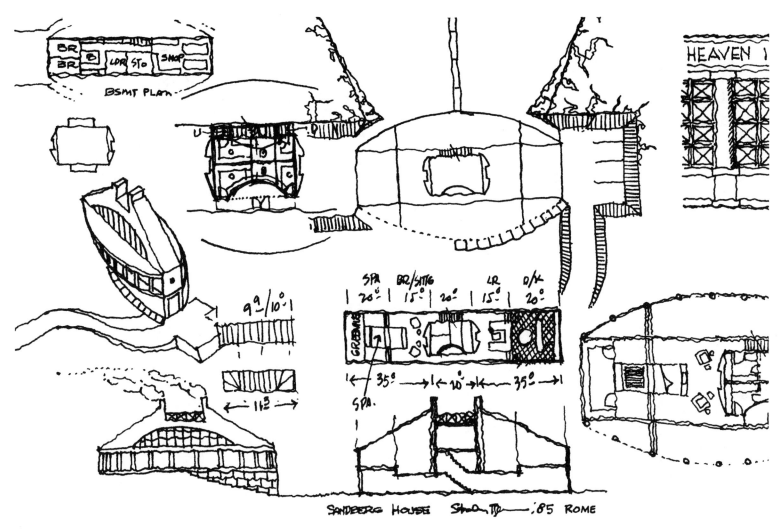

STANLEY TIGERMAN: Study drawing for Sanberg House, Chicago, Illinois, suburb (not built). *Mont Blanc fountain pen on acid-free paper.* [*Courtesy Tigerman McCurry Architects.*]

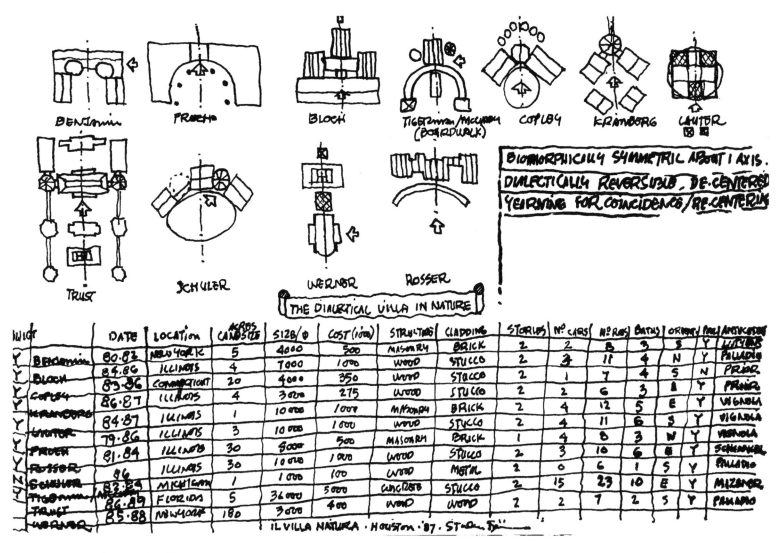

STANLEY TIGERMAN: Analysis of different houses done. *Mont Blanc fountain pen on acid-free paper.* [*Courtesy Tigerman McCurry Architects.*]

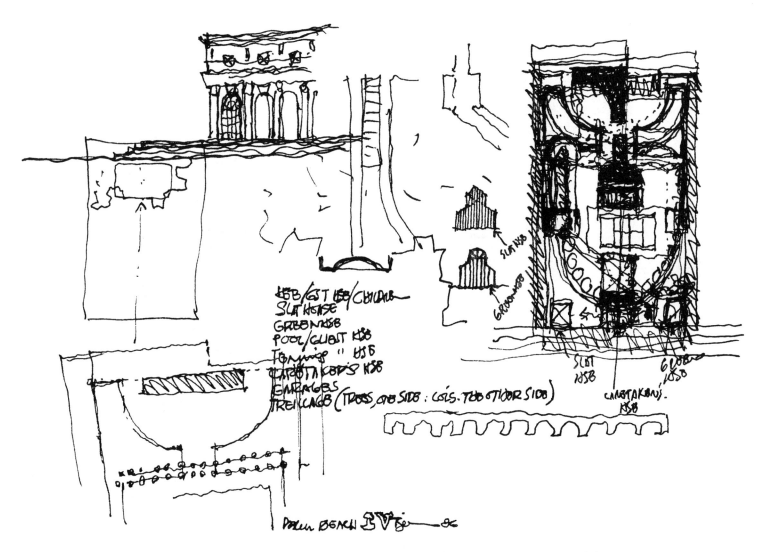

STANLEY TIGERMAN: Study drawing for house in Palm Beach, California. *Mont Blanc fountain pen on acid-free paper.*
[*Courtesy Tigerman McCurry Architects.*]

STANLEY TIGERMAN: Study drawing for Commonwealth Edison, Chicago, Illinois. *Mont Blanc fountain pen on acid-free paper.*
[*Courtesy Tigerman McCurry Architects.*]

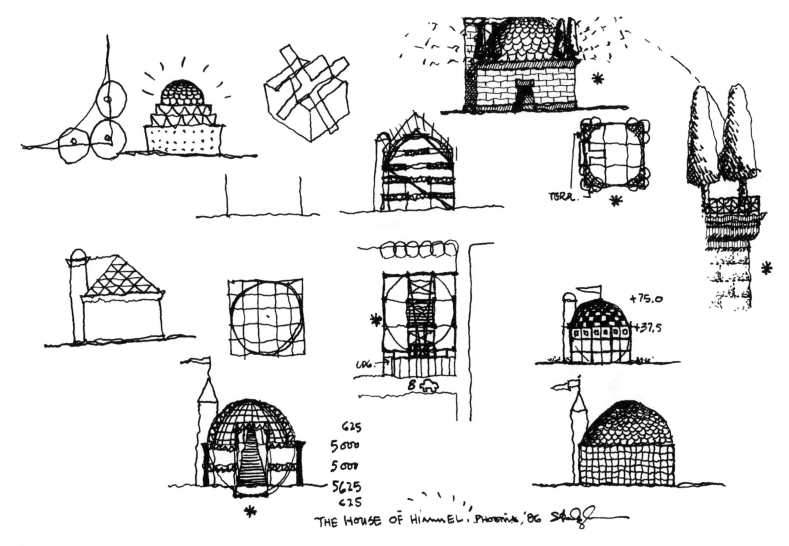

STANLEY TIGERMAN: Study drawing for Richard Himmel House, Chicago, Illinois. *Mont Blanc fountain pen on acid-free paper.*
[*Courtesy Tigerman McCurry Architects.*]

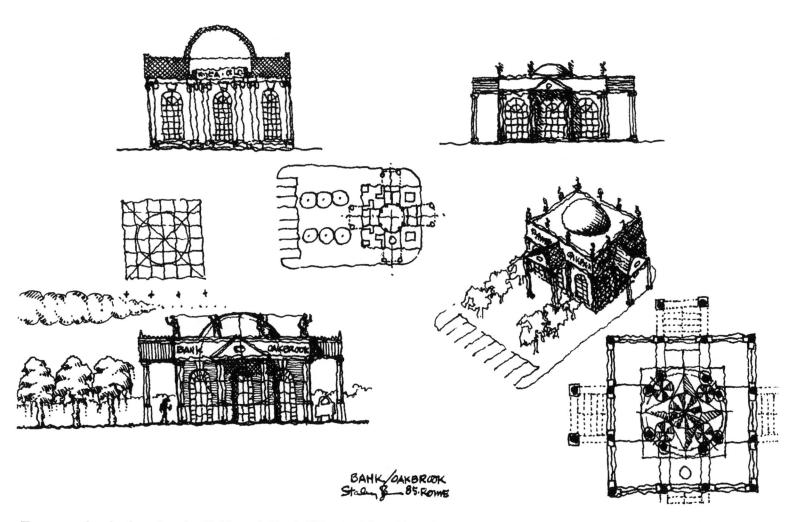

STANLEY TIGERMAN: Study drawing for Oakbrook Bank, Illinois. *Mont Blanc fountain pen on acid-free paper.*
[*Courtesy Tigerman McCurry Architects.*]

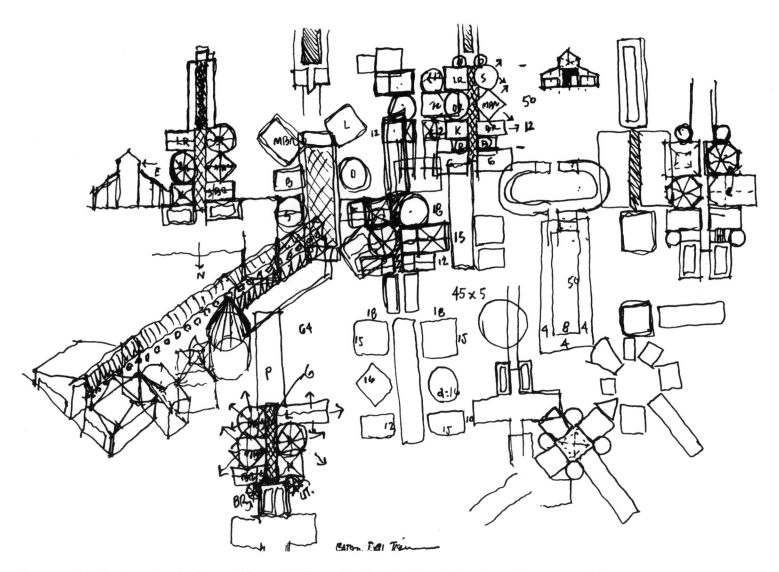

STANLEY TIGERMAN: Study drawing for Eaton House, Indiana (not built). *Mont Blanc fountain pen on acid-free paper.*
[*Courtesy Tigerman McCurry Architects.*]

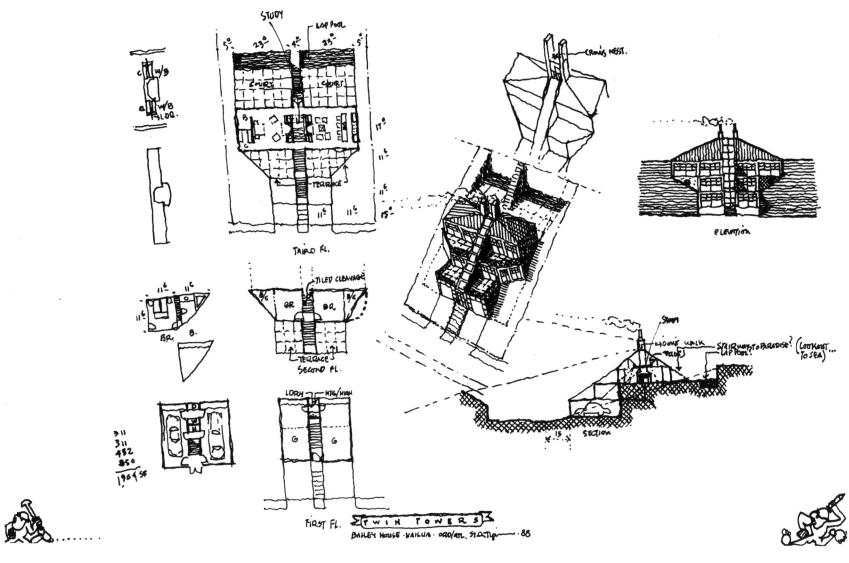

STANLEY TIGERMAN: Study drawing for Bailey House, Kailua, Hawaii (not built). *Mont Blanc fountain pen on acid-free paper.* [*Courtesy Tigerman McCurry Architects.*]

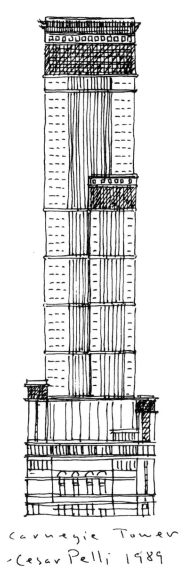

Carnegie Tower
- Cesar Pelli 1989

CESAR PELLI: Study drawing for Carnegie Hall Tower, New York, New York. *Pentel sign pen on sketch paper.*
[*Courtesy Cesar Pelli & Associates Inc. Architects.*]

YCMM   Cesar Pelli '89

CESAR PELLI: Study drawing for Boyer Center for Molecular Medicine, Yale University, New Haven, Connecticut. *Pentel sign pen on sketch paper.* [*Courtesy Cesar Pelli & Associates Inc. Architects.*]

CESAR PELLI: View of World Financial Center and Winter Garden, New York, New York. *Pentel sign pen on sketch paper.*
[*Courtesy Cesar Pelli & Associates Inc. Architects.*]

ALEXIS PONTVIK ARKITEKT: Freehand sketch, competition entry for a skyscraper at Medborgarplatsen in Stockholm, Sweden. *Pilot marker on bond paper.* [*Courtesy Alexis Pontvik Arkitekt (Sweden).*]

FIELD DRAWINGS
IN PEN AND INK

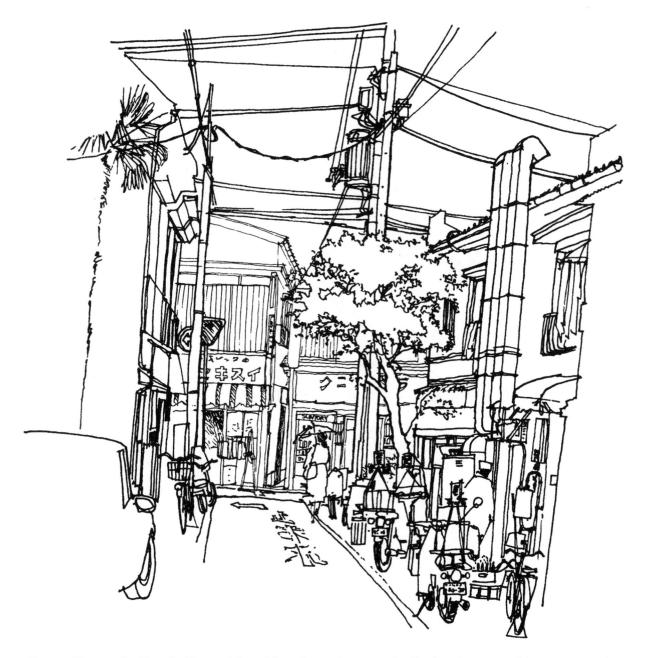

Street in Ookayama, Japan. Drawn by Frank Ching. *Mont Blanc fountain pen on 70 lb. drawing paper.* [*Courtesy Frank Ching.*]

Train station, Jiyugaoka, Japan. Drawn by Frank Ching. *Mont Blanc fountain pen on 70 lb. drawing paper.* [*Courtesy Frank Ching.*]

Goro-tenjinsha Shrine, Ueno Park, Tokyo, Japan. Drawn by Frank Ching. *Mont Blanc fountain pen on 70 lb. drawing paper.*
[*Courtesy Frank Ching.*]

Science Building, Tokodai University, Ookayama, Japan. Drawn by Frank Ching. *Mont Blanc fountain pen on 70 lb. drawing paper.* [*Courtesy Frank Ching.*]

Main street, Ookayama, Japan. Drawn by Frank Ching. *Mont Blanc pen on 70 lb. drawing paper.* [*Courtesy Frank Ching.*]

Detail of Kabuki-za Theater, Tokyo, Japan. Drawn by Frank Ching. *Mont Blanc fountain pen on 70 lb. drawing paper.*
[*Courtesy Frank Ching.*]

Torii leading to Hie Jinja Shrine, Tokyo, Japan. Drawn by Frank Ching. *Mont Blanc fountain pen on 70 lb. drawing paper.*
[*Courtesy Frank Ching.*]

Daibatsu (Great Buddha), Kotokuin Temple, Kamakura, Japan. Drawn by Frank Ching. *Mont Blanc fountain pen on 70 lb. drawing paper.* [*Courtesy Frank Ching.*]

38

Traditional Japanese farmhouse, Hida Folk Village, Takayama, Japan. Drawn by Frank Ching. *Mont Blanc fountain pen on 70 lb. drawing paper.* [*Courtesy Frank Ching.*]

Ninenzaka Slope, Kyoto, Japan. Drawn by Frank Ching. *Mont Blanc fountain pen on 70 lb. drawing paper.* [*Courtesy Frank Ching.*]

Street in Jiyugaoka, Japan. Drawn by Frank Ching. *Mont Blanc fountain pen on 70 lb. drawing paper.* [*Courtesy Frank Ching.*]

Otemon Gate to Imperial Palace, Tokyo, Japan. Drawn by Frank Ching. *Mont Blanc fountain pen on 70 lb. drawing paper.* [*Courtesy Frank Ching.*]

Nijubashi (two-tiered bridge) looking toward Fushimi Yagura, a 17th-century watchtower of the Imperial Palace, Tokyo, Japan. Drawn by Frank Ching. *Mont Blanc fountain pen on 70 lb. drawing paper.* [*Courtesy Frank Ching.*]

Shibuya District, Tokyo, Japan. Drawn by Frank Ching. *Mont Blanc fountain pen on 70 lb. drawing paper.* [*Courtesy Frank Ching.*]

Kaminarimon (Thunder God Gate) leading to Sensoji Temple, Asakusa, Tokyo, Japan. Drawn by Frank Ching. *Mont Blanc fountain pen on 70 lb. drawing paper.* [*Courtesy Frank Ching.*]

Scene from Summer Palace, Beijing, China. Drawn by Yi Gang Peng. *Small nib pen on bond paper.* [*Courtesy Yi Gang Peng (China).*]

Scene from Summer Palace, Beijing, China. Drawn by Yi Gang Peng. *Small nib pen on bond paper.* [*Courtesy Yi Gang Peng (China).*]

Scene from Summer Palace, Beijing, China. Drawn by Yi Gang Peng. *Small nib pen on bond paper.* [*Courtesy Yi Gang Peng (China).*]

Scene from Summer Palace, Beijing, China. Drawn by Yi Gang Peng. *Small nib pen on bond paper.* [*Courtesy Yi Gang Peng (China)*.]

Scene from Summer Palace, Beijing, China. Drawn by Yi Gang Peng. *Small nib pen on bond paper.* [*Courtesy Yi Gang Peng (China).*]

Pavilion, Qianlong Garden, Beijing, China. Drawn by Yi Gang Peng. *Small nib pen on bond paper.* [*Courtesy Yi Gang Peng (China).*]

Scene from Retreat Palace, Chengde, China. Drawn by Yi Gang Peng. *Small nib pen on bond paper.* [*Courtesy Yi Gang Peng (China).*]

Smokey Rain Building, Retreat Palace, Chengde, China. Drawn by Yi Gang Peng. *Small nib pen on bond paper.*
[*Courtesy Yi Gang Peng (China).*]

Scene from Humble Administrator's Garden, Suzhou, China. Drawn by Yi Gang Peng. *Small nib pen on bond paper.* [*Courtesy Yi Gang Peng (China).*]

54

Scene from Humble Administrator's Garden, Suzhou, China. Drawn by Yi Gang Peng. *Small nib pen on bond paper.*
[*Courtesy Yi Gang Peng (China).*]

Scene from Humble Administrator's Garden, Suzhou, China. Drawn by Yi Gang Peng. *Small nib pen on bond paper.*
[*Courtesy Yi Gang Peng (China).*]

Scene from Humble Administrator's Garden, Suzhou, China. Drawn by Yi Gang Peng. *Small nib pen on bond paper.*
[*Courtesy Yi Gang Peng (China).*]

Scene from Humble Administrator's Garden, Suzhou, China. Drawn by Yi Gang Peng. *Small nib pen on bond paper.*
[*Courtesy Yi Gang Peng (China).*]

Scene from Running Tiger Garden, Hangzhou, China. Drawn by Yi Gang Peng. *Small nib pen on bond paper.*
[*Courtesy Yi Gang Peng (China).*]

Scene from Running Tiger Garden, Hangzhou, China. Drawn by Yi Gang Peng. *Small nib pen on bond paper.*
[*Courtesy Yi Gang Peng (China).*]

Scene from Running Tiger Garden, Hangzhou, China. Drawn by Yi Gang Peng. *Small nib pen on bond paper.*
[*Courtesy Yi Gang Peng (China).*]

Scene from Yellow Dragon Cavern, Hangzhou, China. Drawn by Yi Gang Peng. *Small nib pen on bond paper.*
[*Courtesy Yi Gang Peng (China).*]

62

Scene from Yellow Dragon Cavern, Hangzhou, China. Drawn by Yi Gang Peng. *Small nib pen on bond paper.*
[*Courtesy Yi Gang Peng (China).*]

Scene from Carefree Garden, Suzhou, China. Drawn by Yi Gang Peng. *Small nib pen on bond paper.* [*Courtesy Yi Gang Peng (China).*]

Scene from Happy Garden, Suzhou, China. Drawn by Yi Gang Peng. *Small nib pen on bond paper.* [*Courtesy Yi Gang Peng (China).*]

Scene from Crane Garden, Suzhou, China. Drawn by Yi Gang Peng. *Small nib pen on bond paper.* [*Courtesy Yi Gang Peng (China).*]

Scene from Forest of Lions Garden, Suzhou, China. Drawn by Yi Gang Peng. *Small nib pen on bond paper.* [*Courtesy Yi Gang Peng (China).*]

Scene from Retired Fisherman's Garden, Suzhou, China. Drawn by Yi Gang Peng. *Small nib pen on bond paper.*
[*Courtesy Yi Gang Peng (China).*]

Scene from Retired Fisherman's Garden, Suzhou, China. Drawn by Yi Gang Peng. *Small nib pen on bond paper.*
[*Courtesy Yi Gang Peng (China).*]

Scene from Lingering-Here Garden, Suzhou, China. Drawn by Yi Gang Peng. *Small nib pen on bond paper.*
[*Courtesy Yi Gang Peng (China).*]

Scene from Lingering-Here Garden, Suzhou, China. Drawn by Yi Gang Peng. *Small nib pen on bond paper.*
[*Courtesy Yi Gang Peng (China).*]

Scene from Lingering-Here Garden, Suzhou, China. Drawn by Yi Gang Peng. *Small nib pen on bond paper.*
[*Courtesy Yi Gang Peng (China).*]

72

Scene from Lingering-Here Garden, Suzhou, China. Drawn by Yi Gang Peng. *Small nib pen on bond paper.*
[*Courtesy Yi Gang Peng (China).*]

Al Zabrek House, Bethesda, Maryland. Drawn by John S. M. Chen. *Pilot Fineliner felt pen on vellum.* [*Courtesy John S. M. Chen.*]

Al Zabrek House, Bethesda, Maryland. Drawn by John S. M. Chen. *Pilot Fineliner felt pen on vellum.* [*Courtesy John S. M. Chen.*]

Main gate, Howard University, Washington, D.C. Drawn by John S. M. Chen. *Pilot Fineliner felt pen on xerox paper.*
[*Courtesy John S. M. Chen.*]

76

Andrew Rankin Chapel, Howard University, Washington, D.C. Drawn by John S. M. Chen. *Pilot Fineliner felt pen on xerox paper.* [*Courtesy John S. M. Chen.*]

Founders Library, Howard University, Washington, D.C. Drawn by John S. M. Chen. *Pilot Fineliner felt pen on xerox paper.*
[*Courtesy John S. M. Chen.*]

Reading room, Founders Library, Howard University, Washington, D.C. Drawn by John S. M. Chen. *Pilot Fineliner felt pen on xerox paper.* [*Courtesy John S. M. Chen.*]

School of Architecture and Planning, Howard University, Washington, D.C. Drawn by John S. M. Chen. *Pilot Fineliner felt pen on xerox paper.* [*Courtesy John S. M. Chen.*]

East Wing, National Gallery of Arts, Washington, D.C. Drawn by John S. M. Chen. *Technical pen on vellum.* [*Courtesy John S. M. Chen.*]

Falling Water, Bear Run, Pennsylvania. Drawn by John S. M. Chen. *Nib pen on vellum.* [*Courtesy John S. M. Chen.*]

Ruins of Yuan Ming Gardens, Beijing, China. Drawn by John S. M. Chen. *Nib pen on vellum.* [*Courtesy John S. M. Chen.*]

Ruins of Yuan Ming Gardens, Beijing, China. Drawn by John S. M. Chen. *Nib pen on vellum.* [*Courtesy John S. M. Chen.*]

Archway, Vezelay, France. Drawn by Robert Lewicki. *Pilot Fineliner felt pen on bond paper.* [*Courtesy Robert Lewicki (Canada).*]

ST. PHILIBERT, TOURNUS ©90 R. LEWICKI

St. Philibert, Tournus, France. Drawn by Robert Lewicki. *Pilot Fineliner felt pen on bond paper.* [*Courtesy Robert Lewicki (Canada).*]

86

Clocktower, Auxerre, France. Drawn by Robert Lewicki. *Pilot Fineliner felt pen on bond paper.* [*Courtesy Robert Lewicki (Canada).*]

St. Mary's Church, Newton, Massachusetts. Drawn by Paul Stevenson Oles. *Technical pen, fountain pen on watercolor paper.*
[*Courtesy Paul Stevenson Oles.*]

"Winter Home," Newton, Massachusetts. Drawn by Paul Stevenson Oles. *Technical pen on vellum.* [*Courtesy Paul Stevenson Oles.*]

Villa Pio Vatican Garden, Rome, Italy. Drawn by Stanley Tigerman. *Mont Blanc fountain pen on acid-free paper.* [*Courtesy Tigerman McCurry Architects.*]

Franklin School, Board of Education, Washington, D.C. Drawn by Richard Fitzhugh. *Technical pen on bond paper.*
[*Courtesy Richard Fitzhugh.*]

PRESENTATION DRAWINGS
IN PEN AND INK

PAUL RUDOLPH ARCHITECT: Bond Centre, Hong Kong. Drawn by Paul Rudolph Architect. *Technical pen on vellum.* [*Courtesy Paul Rudolph.*]

PAUL RUDOLPH ARCHITECT: Bond Centre, Hong Kong. Drawn by Paul Rudolph Architect. *Technical pen on vellum.* [*Courtesy Paul Rudolph.*]

PAUL RUDOLPH ARCHITECT: Bond Centre, Hong Kong. Drawn by Paul Rudolph Architect. *Technical pen on vellum.* [*Courtesy Paul Rudolph.*]

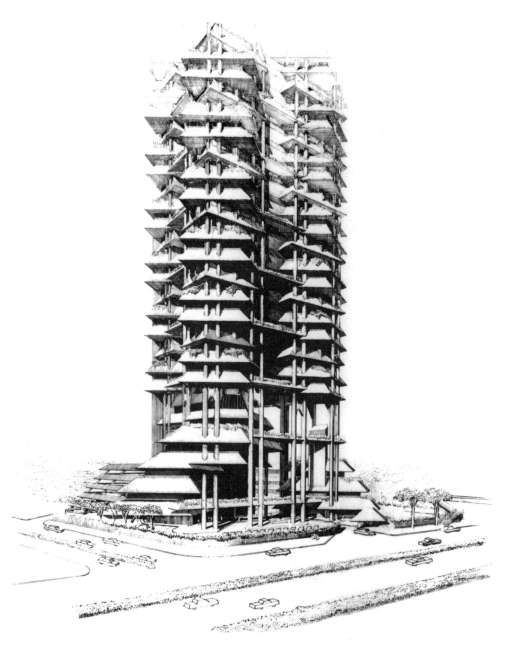

PAUL RUDOLPH ARCHITECT: Dharmala Office Building, Jakarta, Indonesia. Drawn by Paul Rudolph Architect. *Technical pen on vellum.*
[*Courtesy Paul Rudolph.*]

PAUL RUDOLPH ARCHITECT: Dharmala Office Building, Jakarta, Indonesia. Drawn by Paul Rudolph Architect. *Technical pen on vellum.* [*Courtesy Paul Rudolph.*]

PAUL RUDOLPH ARCHITECT: Dharmala Office Building, Jakarta, Indonesia. Drawn by Paul Rudolph Architect. *Technical pen on vellum.* [*Courtesy Paul Rudolph.*]

100

PAUL RUDOLPH ARCHITECT: Dharmala Office Building, Jakarta, Indonesia. Drawn by Paul Rudolph Architect. *Technical pen on vellum.*
[*Courtesy Paul Rudolph.*]

PAUL RUDOLPH ARCHITECT: Colonnade Condominiums, Grange Road, Singapore. Drawn by Paul Rudolph Architect. *Technical pen on vellum.*
[*Courtesy Paul Rudolph.*]

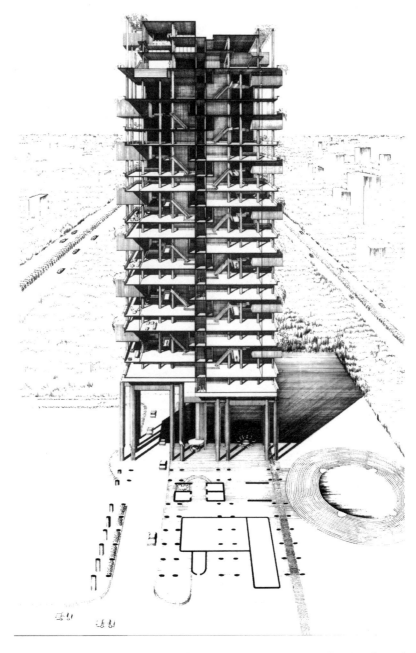

PAUL RUDOLPH ARCHITECT: Colonnade Condominiums, Grange Road, Singapore. Drawn by Paul Rudolph Architect. *Technical pen on vellum.*
[*Courtesy Paul Rudolph.*]

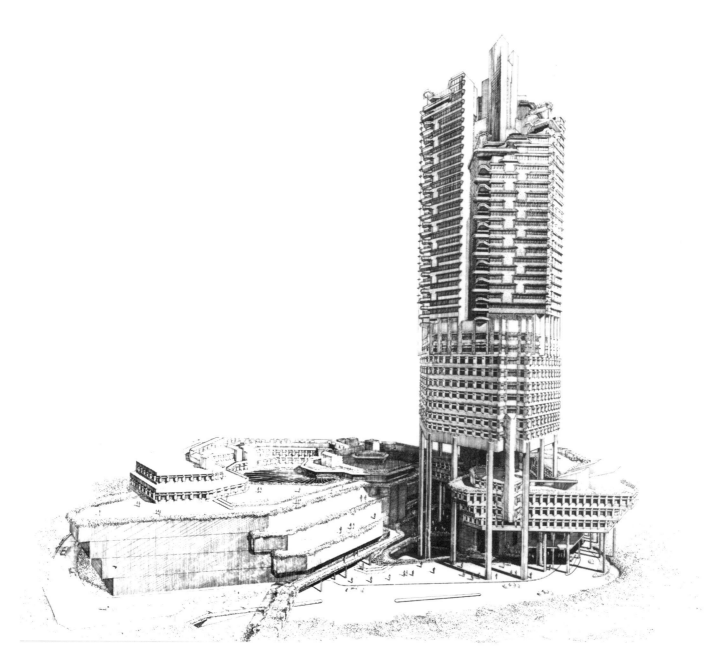

PAUL RUDOLPH ARCHITECT: Beach Road #1 (not built), Singapore. Drawn by Paul Rudolph Architect. *Technical pen on vellum.* [*Courtesy Paul Rudolph.*]

104

PAUL RUDOLPH ARCHITECT: Burroughs-Wellcome Cafeteria, Triangle Park, North Carolina. Drawn by Paul Rudolph Architect. *Technical pen on vellum.* [*Courtesy Paul Rudolph.*]

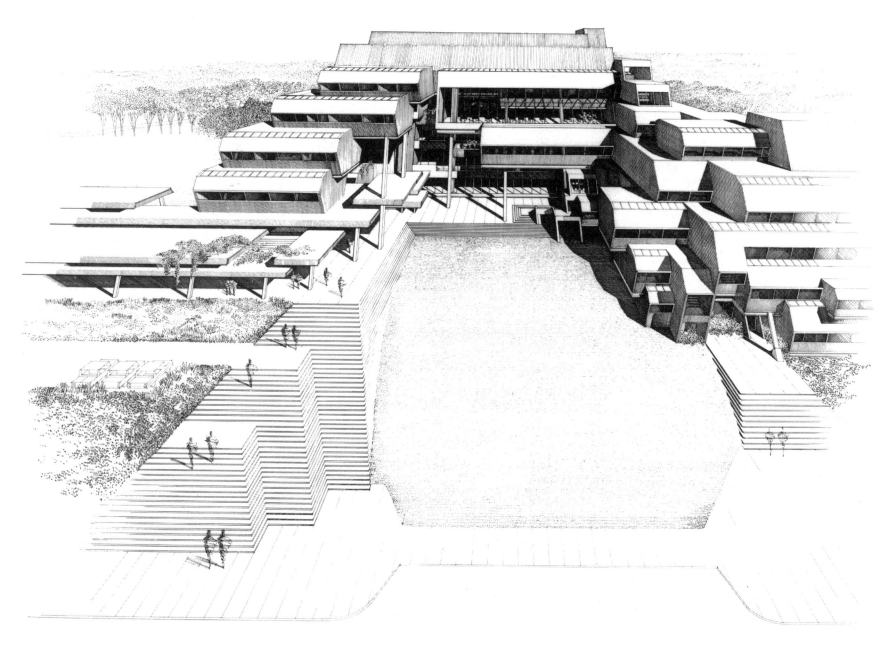

PAUL RUDOLPH ARCHITECT: Burroughs-Wellcome, Triangle Park, North Carolina. Drawn by Paul Rudolph Architect. *Technical pen on vellum.* [*Courtesy Paul Rudolph.*]

PAUL RUDOLPH ARCHITECT: Yale School of Art and Architecture, New Haven, Connecticut. Drawn by Paul Rudolph Architect. *Technical pen on vellum.* [*Courtesy Paul Rudolph.*]

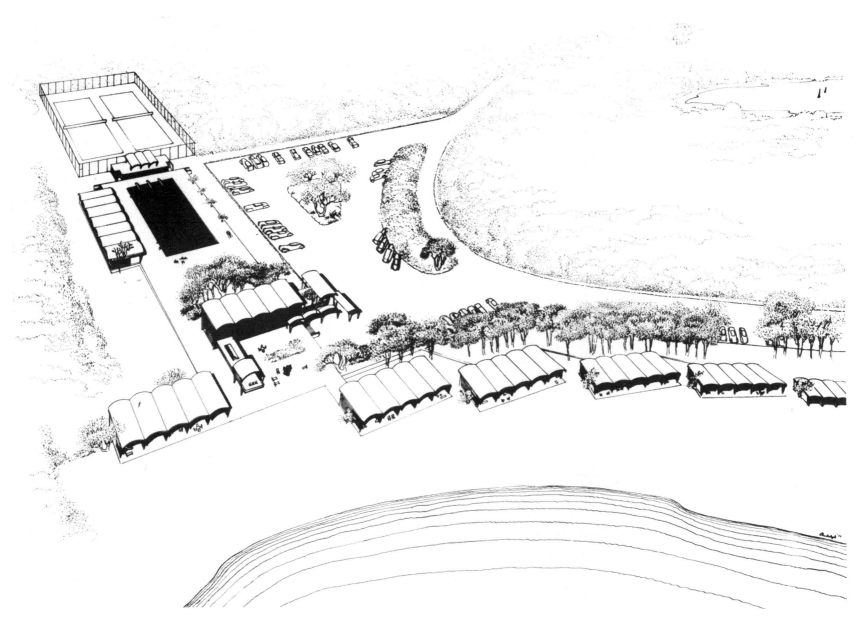

PAUL RUDOLPH ARCHITECT: Sandering Beach Club, Siesta Key, Florida. Drawn by Paul Rudolph Architect. *Technical pen on vellum.* [*Courtesy Paul Rudolph.*]

PAUL RUDOLPH ARCHITECT: Knott Residence, Yankeetown, Florida. Drawn by Paul Rudolph Architect. *Technical pen on vellum.* [*Courtesy Paul Rudolph.*]

Paul Rudolph Architect: Oriental Masonic Gardens Housing, New Haven, Connecticut. Drawn by Paul Rudolph Architect. *Technical pen on vellum.* [*Courtesy Paul Rudolph.*]

Murphy/Jahn Inc. Architects: Office building, Stuttgart, Germany. Drawn by Rael D. Slutsky & Associates. *Felt pen on vellum.*
[*Courtesy Rael D. Slutsky.*]

MURPHY/JAHN INC. AND O'HARE ASSOCIATES ARCHITECTS: United Airlines Terminal, O'Hare International Airport, Chicago, Illinois. Drawn by Rael D. Slutsky & Associates. *Technical pen on mylar.* [*Courtesy Rael D. Slutsky.*]

Murphy/Jahn Inc. and O'Hare Associates Architects: United Airlines Terminal, O'Hare International Airport, Chicago, Illinois. Drawn by Rael D. Slutsky & Associates. *Technical pen on mylar.* [*Courtesy Rael D. Slutsky.*]

PERKINS & WILL ARCHITECTS: Morton International Building, Chicago, Illinois. Drawn by Rael D. Slutsky & Associates. *Technical pen on mylar.* [*Courtesy Rael D. Slutsky.*]

PERKINS & WILL ARCHITECTS: Morton International Building, Chicago, Illinois. Drawn by Rael D. Slutsky & Associates. *Technical pen, felt pen on vellum.* [*Courtesy Rael D. Slutsky.*]

SKIDMORE, OWINGS AND MERRILL: One North Franklin, Chicago, Illinois. Drawn by Rael D. Slutsky & Associates. *Felt pen on vellum.*
[*Courtesy Rael D. Slutsky.*]

116

SKIDMORE, OWINGS AND MERRILL/GRAHAM GUND ARCHITECTS: 75 State Street, Boston, Massachusetts. Drawn by Rael D. Slutsky & Associates. *Technical pen on mylar.* [*Courtesy Rael D. Slutsky.*]

SKIDMORE, OWINGS AND MERRILL: Lyric Opera of Chicago, new storage/staging, Chicago, Illinois. Drawn by Rael D. Slutsky & Associates. *Technical pen on mylar. [Courtesy Rael D. Slutsky.]*

SKIDMORE, OWINGS AND MERRILL: Bishops Gate, Phase 9/10, London, England. Drawn by Rael D. Slutsky & Associates. *Technical pen, felt pen on vellum.* [*Courtesy Rael D. Slutsky.*]

119

SOLOMON CORDWELL BUENZ: National Home Furnishing Institute, Chicago, Illinois. Drawn by Rael D. Slutsky & Associates. *Felt pen on vellum.* [*Courtesy Rael D. Slutsky.*]

GRAHAM, PROBST, ANDERSON & WHITE: The Civic Opera House for the Lyric Opera of Chicago, Chicago, Illinois.
Drawn by Rael D. Slutsky & Associates. *Technical pen on mylar.* [*Courtesy Rael D. Slutsky.*]

ROY H. KRUSE & ASSOCIATES: The Point Townhomes, Chicago, Illinois. Drawn by Rael D. Slutsky & Associates. *Technical pen on mylar.* [*Courtesy Rael D. Slutsky.*]

HOLABIRD & ROOT: Chicago Historical Society, Chicago, Illinois. Drawn by Rael D. Slutsky & Associates. *Technical pen on mylar.*
[*Courtesy Rael D. Slutsky.*]

PEI COBB FREED ARCHITECTS: First Bank Place, Minneapolis, Minnesota. Drawn by Rael D. Slutsky & Associates. *Technical pen on mylar.* [*Courtesy Rael D. Slutsky.*]

124

HartMan Cox Architects: 1501 M Street Building, Washington, D.C. Drawn by John Chen Studio. *Technical pen on mylar.*
[*Courtesy Kossow Development Corporation.*]

HARTMAN COX ARCHITECTS: 1501 M Street Building, Washington, D.C. Drawn by John Chen Studio. *Technical pen on mylar.*
[*Courtesy Kossow Development Corporation.*]

126

HARTMAN COX ARCHITECTS: 1501 M Street Building, Washington, D.C. Drawn by John Chen Studio. *Technical pen on mylar.*
[*Courtesy Kossow Development Corporation.*]

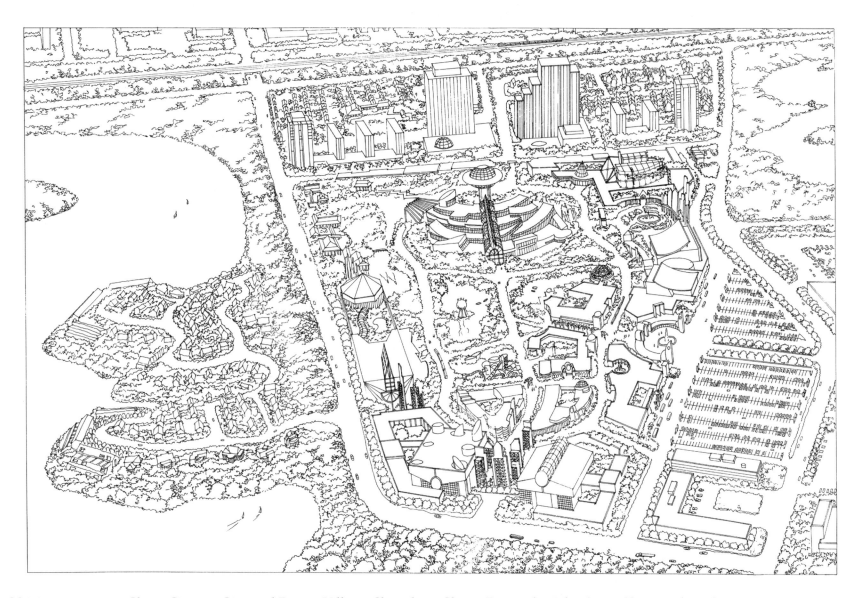

CSR International: China Cinema City and Resort Village, Shenzhen, China. Drawn by John S. M. Chen. *Technical pen on mylar.*
[*Courtesy John S. M. Chen.*]

ASHLEY GROUP: Townhouse, Baltimore County, Maryland. Drawn by John Chen Studio. *Technical pen on mylar.* [*Courtesy John S. M. Chen.*]

ASHLEY GROUP: Townhouse, Baltimore County, Maryland. Drawn by John Chen Studio. *Technical pen on mylar.* [*Courtesy John S. M. Chen.*]

CLEMENT CHEN & ASSOCIATES: Jianguo Hotel, Beijing, China. Drawn by John S. M. Chen. *Technical pen on vellum.* [*Courtesy John S. M. Chen.*]

131

LOHAN ASSOCIATES, ARCHITECTS: Burlington Headquarters Competition, Texas. Drawn by Gilbert Gorski. *Technical pen on vellum.* [*Courtesy Gilbert Gorski.*]

LOHAN ASSOCIATES, ARCHITECTS: Burlington Headquarters Competition, Texas. Drawn by Gilbert Gorski. *Technical pen on vellum.*
[*Courtesy Gilbert Gorski.*]

LOHAN ASSOCIATES, ARCHITECTS: Am South Headquarters, Georgia. Drawn by Gilbert Gorski. *Koh-i-noor Rapidograph pen on clearprint paper.* [*Courtesy Gilbert Gorski.*]

LOHAN ASSOCIATES, ARCHITECTS: Am South Headquarters, Georgia. Drawn by Gilbert Gorski. *Koh-i-noor Rapidograph pen on clearprint paper.* [*Courtesy Gilbert Gorski.*]

LOHAN ASSOCIATES, ARCHITECTS: Am South Headquarters, Georgia. Drawn by Gilbert Gorski. *Koh-i-noor Rapidograph pen on clearprint paper.* [*Courtesy Gilbert Gorski.*]

136

LOHAN ASSOCIATES, ARCHITECTS: **Prairie Cove, Pleasant Prairie, Wisconsin. Drawn by Gilbert Gorski.** *Technical pen on vellum.*
[*Courtesy Gilbert Gorski.*]

ANTUNOVICH ASSOCIATES, ARCHITECTS: O'Hare West Office Campus, Des Plaines, Illinois. Drawn by Gilbert Gorski. *Koh-i-noor Rapidograph pen on clearprint paper.* [*Courtesy Gilbert Gorski.*]

Antunovich Associates, Architects: Interior view, Des Plaines Office Center, Des Plaines, Illinois. Drawn by Gilbert Gorski. *Technical pen on vellum.* [*Courtesy Gilbert Gorski.*]

"Michigan Avenue at the River," Chicago, Illinois. Drawn by Gilbert Gorski. *Koh-i-noor Rapidograph pen on clearprint paper.*
[*Courtesy Gilbert Gorski.*]

140

HOK New York: Somerset Development, Somerset, New Jersey. Drawn by Gilbert Gorski. *Koh-i-noor Rapidograph pen on clearprint paper.* [*Courtesy Gilbert Gorski.*]

141

Colosseum, Rome, Italy. Drawn by Gilbert Gorski. *Crow quill pen on bond paper.* [*Courtesy Gilbert Gorski.*]

PERKINS & HAMILTON 1908: Cafe Brauer (South Pond Refectory), Chicago, Illinois. Drawn by Gilbert Gorski. *Technical pen on vellum.* [*Courtesy Gilbert Gorski.*]

PERKINS & WILL ARCHITECTS: L.U.M.C. Cancer Research Center, Maywood, Illinois. Drawn by Manuel Avila. *Technical pen on vellum.* [*Courtesy Manuel Avila.*]

PERKINS & WILL ARCHITECTS: L.U.M.C. Cancer Research Center, Maywood, Illinois. Drawn by Manuel Avila. *Technical pen on vellum.* [*Courtesy Manuel Avila.*]

PERKINS & WILL ARCHITECTS: GSA, IRS Competition, suburban Pittsburgh, Pennsylvania. Drawn by Manual Avila. *Technical pen on vellum.* [*Courtesy Manuel Avila.*]

PERKINS & WILL ARCHITECTS: GSA, IRS Competition, suburban Pittsburgh, Pennsylvania. Drawn by Manuel Avila. *Technical pen on vellum.*
[*Courtesy Manuel Avila.*]

PERKINS & WILL ARCHITECTS: Thomson Consumer Electronics, Indianapolis, Indiana. Drawn by Manuel Avila. *Technical pen on vellum.* [*Courtesy Manuel Avila.*]

PERKINS & WILL ARCHITECTS: Dongbu Central, South Korea. Drawn by Manuel Avila. *Technical pen on vellum.* [*Courtesy Manuel Avila.*]

PERKINS & WILL ARCHITECTS: Edges Systems, Chicago, Illinois. Drawn by Manuel Avila. *Technical pen on vellum.* [*Courtesy Manuel Avila.*]

150

VLECIDES & SCHROEDER ARCHITECTS: P.R.T. Station Matrix, suburban Chicago, Illinois. Drawn by Manuel Avila. *Technical pen on vellum.*
[*Courtesy Manuel Avila.*]

151

KNIGHT ARCHITECTS: Main Post Office Building, Chicago, Illinois. Drawn by Manuel Avila. *Technical pen on vellum.* [*Courtesy Manuel Avila.*]

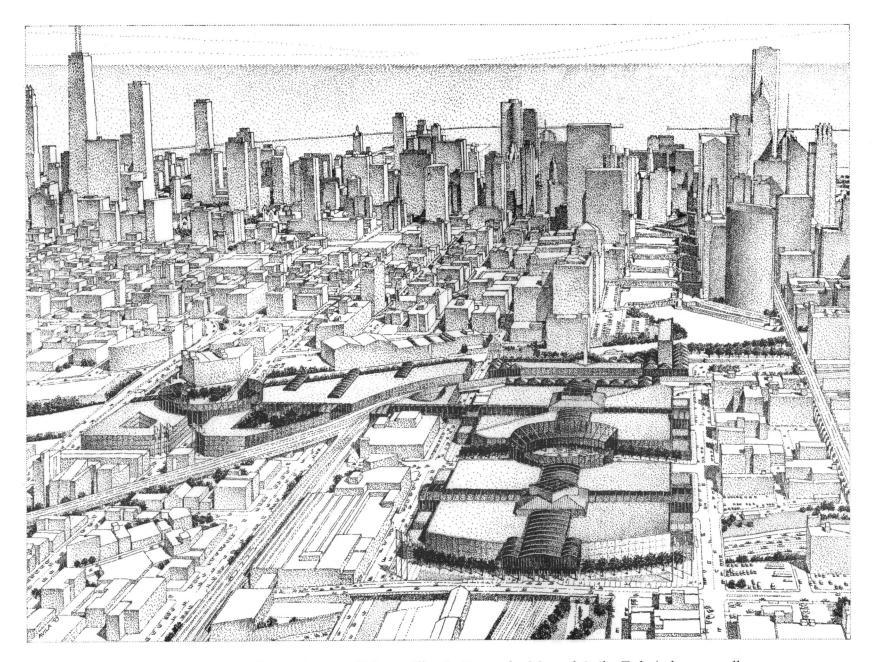

LOHAN ASSOCIATES, ARCHITECTS: Casino + Entertainment, Chicago, Illinois. Drawn by Manuel Avila. *Technical pen on vellum.*
[*Courtesy Manuel Avila.*]

HELLMUTH, OBATA & KASSABAUM: Amtrak Station proposal, New York. Drawn by Manuel Avila. *Technical pen on vellum.*
[*Courtesy Manuel Avila.*]

154

HELLMUTH, OBATA & KASSABAUM: JFK Terminal One Competition, New York. Drawn by Manuel Avila. *Technical pen with prismacolor pencils on vellum.* [*Courtesy Manuel Avila.*]

ENGINEERING MANAGEMENT CONSULTANTS: Union Station, Los Angeles, California. Drawn by Gene Streett. *Technical pen on vellum.*
[*Courtesy Gene Streett.*]

ENGINEERING MANAGEMENT CONSULTANTS: 7th/Flower Station, Los Angeles, California. Drawn by Gene Streett. *Technical pen on vellum.* [*Courtesy Gene Streett.*]

ENGINEERING MANAGEMENT CONSULTANTS: 7th/Flower Station, Los Angeles, California. Drawn by Gene Streett. *Technical pen on vellum.* [*Courtesy Gene Streett.*]

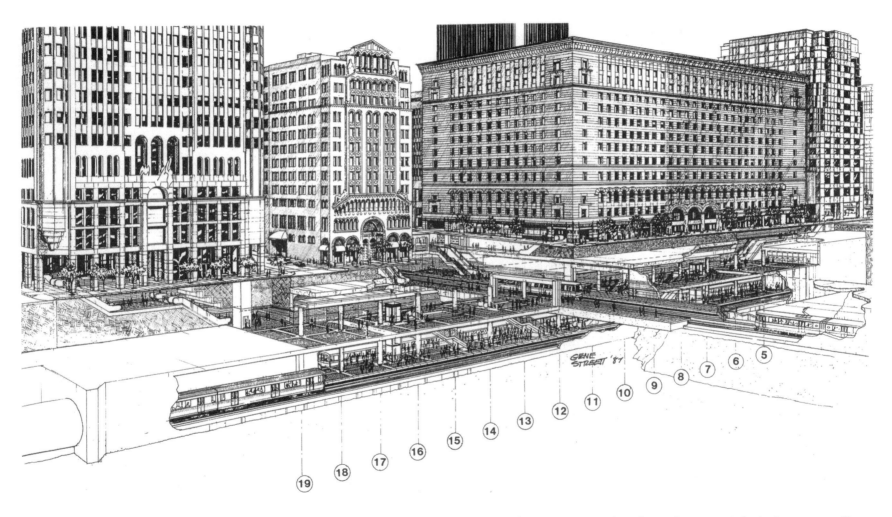

ENGINEERING MANAGEMENT CONSULTANTS: 7th/Flower Station, Los Angeles, California. Drawn by Gene Streett. *Technical pen on vellum.*
[*Courtesy Gene Streett.*]

ENGINEERING MANAGEMENT CONSULTANTS: Union Station, Los Angeles, California. Drawn by Gene Streett. *Technical pen on vellum.* [*Courtesy Gene Streett.*]

160

ENGINEERING MANAGEMENT CONSULTANTS: Fairfax/Santa Monica Station, Hollywood, California. Drawn by Gene Streett. *Technical pen on vellum.* [*Courtesy Gene Streett.*]

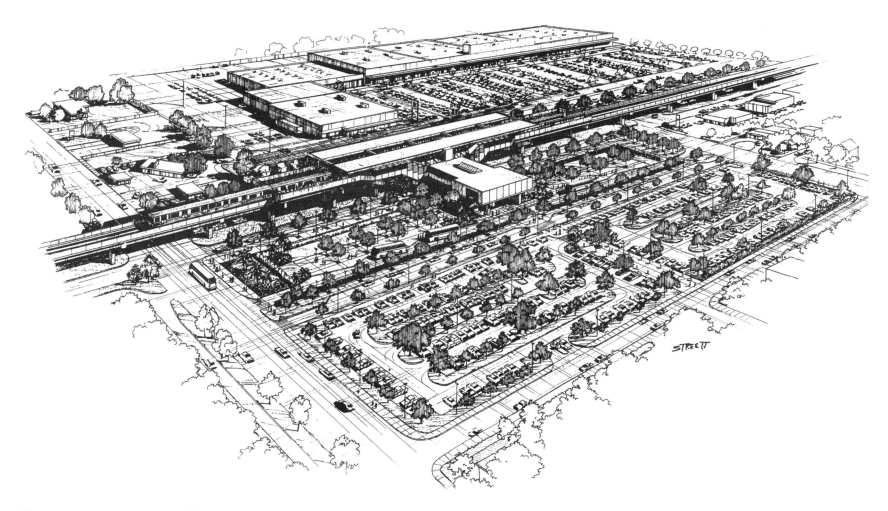

HARRY WEESE & ASSOCIATES: Northside Station, Miami, Florida. Drawn by Gene Streett. *Technical pen on vellum.* [*Courtesy Gene Streett.*]

Zᴇɪᴅʟᴇʀ Rᴏʙᴇʀᴛs Pᴀʀᴛɴᴇʀsʜɪᴘ: Deerhurst Highlands Condominium Village, Huntsville, Ontario, Canada. Drawn by Gordon Grice & Associates. *Technical pen on mylar.* [*Courtesy Gordon Grice (Canada).*]

ZEIDLER ROBERTS PARTNERSHIP: Deerhurst Highlands Unit A, Huntsville, Ontario, Canada. Drawn by Gordon Grice & Associates. *Technical pen on mylar.* [*Courtesy Gordon Grice (Canada).*]

ZEIDLER ROBERTS PARTNERSHIP: Deerhurst Highlands Unit C, Huntsville, Ontario, Canada. Drawn by Gordon Grice & Associates. *Technical pen on mylar. [Courtesy Gordon Grice (Canada).]*

McDonnell Douglas/EDS: The Reality of Infrastructure Management. Drawn by Gordon Grice & Associates. *Technical pen on mylar.* [*Courtesy Gordon Grice (Canada).*]

WEBB ZERAFA MENKES HOUSDEN/KEITH LOFFLER: King Abdulaziz University, Jeddah, Saudi Arabia. Drawn by Gordon Grice & Associates. *Technical pen on mylar. [Courtesy Gordon Grice (Canada).]*

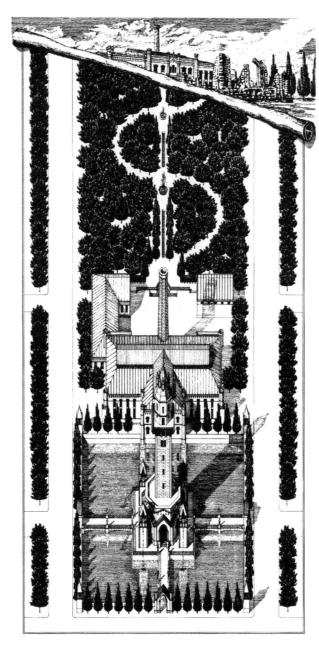

THOMAS NORMAN RAJKOVICH, ARCHITECT: Project for the Reconstruction of the Chicago Water Works Tower and Adjacent Gardens, Chicago, Illinois. Drawn by Thomas Norman Rajkovich. *Crow quill pen on museum board.* [*Courtesy Thomas Norman Rajkovich, Architect.*]

168

PAUL MERRICK ARCHITECTS LTD.: Apartment Tower Competition, Singapore. Drawn by Ronald J. Love. *Koh-i-noor Rapidograph pen on Strathmore drawing paper.* [*Courtesy Ronald J. Love (Canada).*]

<small>Dalla-Lana/Griffin Architects: Ambulatory Care Center, Vancouver General Hospital, Canada. Drawn by Ronald J. Love.
Koh-i-noor Rapidograph pen on Strathmore drawing paper. [*Courtesy Ronald J. Love (Canada).*]</small>

170

Artist concept of Manhattan Island's World Financial Center and Battery Park City, New York. Drawn by John Stuart Pryce. *Technical pen on vellum.* [*Courtesy John Stuart Pryce (Canada).*]

HOH Associates: Long Meade at Port Tobacco, Charles County, Maryland. Drawn by Richard Fitzhugh. *Technical pen on illustration board.*
[*Courtesy Richard Fitzhugh.*]

HUGH NEWELL JACOBSEN, FAIA, ARCHITECT: Knapp House, Southern California. Drawn by Howard Associates. *Technical pen on bond paper.* [*Courtesy Howard Associates.*]

Hugh Newell Jacobsen, FAIA, Architect: Mountain Villa, Athens, Greece. Drawn by Howard Associates. *Technical pen on bond paper.* [*Courtesy Howard Associates.*]

Hugh Newell Jacobsen, FAIA, Architects: Garner House, Santa Ynez Valley, California. Drawn by Howard Associates. *Technical pen on bond paper.* [*Courtesy Howard Associates.*]

HUGH NEWELL JACOBSEN, FAIA, ARCHITECT: Segal House, Florida. Drawn by Howard Associates. *Technical pen on bond paper.*
[*Courtesy Howard Associates.*]

MICELI KULIK WILLIAMS & ASSOCIATES, P.C., LANDSCAPE ARCHITECTS: Cunningham Park, Queens, New York. Drawn by Howard Associates. *Technical pen on bond paper.* [*Courtesy Howard Associates.*]

Miceli Kulik Williams & Associates, P.C., Landscape Architects: Commercial Development, Longswamp Wetland Migration, Palisades Park, New Jersey. Drawn by Howard Associates. *Technical pen on bond paper.* [*Courtesy Howard Associates.*]

RTKL Associates, Inc.: U.S. Embassy, Kuwait. Drawn by Howard Associates. *Technical pen on bond paper.* [*Courtesy Howard Associates.*]

RTKL Associates, Inc.: Master plan, George Washington University, University Center, Loudoun County, Virginia. Drawn by Howard Associates. *Technical pen on bond paper.* [*Courtesy Howard Associates.*]

180

RTKL Associates, Inc.: Design study, Visitors Center, U.S. Capitol, Washington, D.C. Drawn by Howard Associates. *Technical pen on bond paper. [Courtesy Howard Associates.]*

Bauer Stark + Lashbrook: Landmark re-use study, Ford Estate, Perrysburg, Ohio. Drawn by Howard Associates. *Technical pen on Strathmore board.* [*Courtesy Howard Associates.*]

ENVIRONMENTAL PLANNING & DESIGN: Boxwood Garden, Missouri Botanical Garden, Saint Louis, Missouri. Drawn by Howard Associates. *Technical pen on bond paper. [Courtesy Howard Associates.]*

LUCKENBACH/ZIEGELMAN AND PARTNERS INC., ARCHITECTS: American Concrete Institute corporate offices, Farmington Hills, Michigan. Drawn by Howard Associates. *Technical pen on bond paper.* [*Courtesy Howard Associates.*]

V<small>LASTIMIL</small> K<small>OUBEK</small>, AIA, A<small>RCHITECT</small>: Willard Hotel, Washington, D.C. Drawn by Howard Associates. *Technical pen on bond paper.*
[*Courtesy Howard Associates.*]

ROBERT CARL WILLIAMS, AIA, ARCHITECT: Sunrise Mountain Condominiums, Vermont. Drawn by Howard Associates. *Technical pen on bond paper.* [*Courtesy Howard Associates.*]

EMERY ROTH & SONS, P.C., HARDY HOLSMAN PFEIFFER ASSOCIATES, HOOKER/SISKIND & ASSOCIATES INC.: Ferry Landing competition entry, New York City. Drawn by Howard Associates. *Technical pen on bond paper.* [*Courtesy Howard Associates.*]

QUINLIVAN PIERIK & KRAUSE ARCHITECTS: James K. Herbert Alumni Center, United States Military Academy, West Point, New York. Drawn by Howard Associates. *Technical pen on Strathmore board. [Courtesy Howard Associates.]*

DEVROUAX & PURNELL IN ASSOCIATION WITH SKIDMORE, OWENS & MERRILL AND EDAW: "Proposed" Black Patriots Memorial, Washington, D.C. Drawn by Howard Associates. *Technical pen on Strathmore board.* [*Courtesy Howard Associates.*]

SKIDMORE, OWINGS & MERRILL: Mixed-Use Development Center, New Haven, Connecticut. Drawn by Howard Associates. *Technical pen on bond paper.* [*Courtesy Howard Associates.*]

190

JAMES STEWART POLSHEK & PARTNERS, ARCHITECTS: Akron Convention Center, Akron, Ohio. Drawn by Howard Associates. *Technical pen on bond paper.* [*Courtesy Howard Associates.*]

JOHN BURGEE ARCHITECTS WITH PHILIP JOHNSON: Atlantic Center, Atlanta, Georgia. Drawn by Howard Associates. *Technical pen on Strathmore board.* [*Courtesy Howard Associates.*]

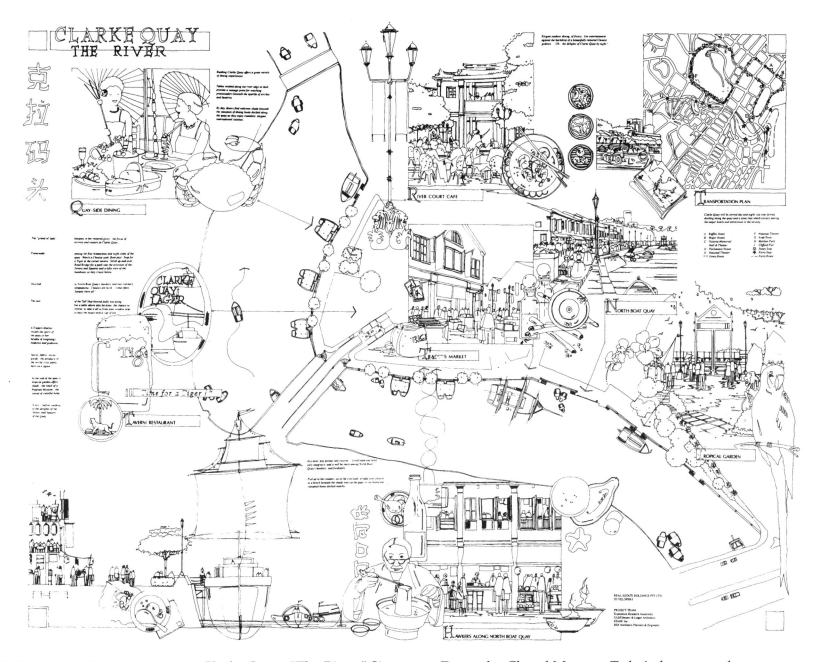

ELS/ELBASANI & LOGAN ARCHITECTS: Clarke Quay, "The River," Singapore. Drawn by Cheryl Morgan. *Technical pen on mylar.*
[*Courtesy Cheryl Morgan.*]

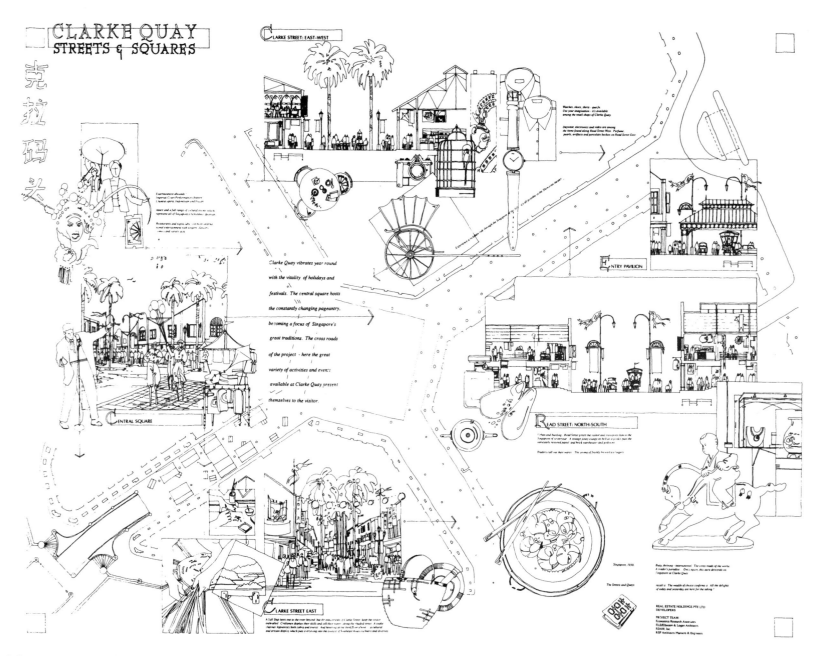

ELS/ELBASANI & LOGAN ARCHITECTS: Clarke Quay, "Streets and Squares", Singapore. Drawn by Cheryl Morgan. *Technical pen on mylar.*
[*Courtesy Cheryl Morgan.*]

ALEXIS PONTVIK ARKITEKT: The Swedish Pavilion for the International Exhibition of 11 cities and 11 nations in Leeuwarden, The Netherlands. Drawn by Alexis Pontvik Arkitekt. *Technical pen on polyester film.* [*Courtesy Alexis Pontvik Arkitekt (Sweden).*]

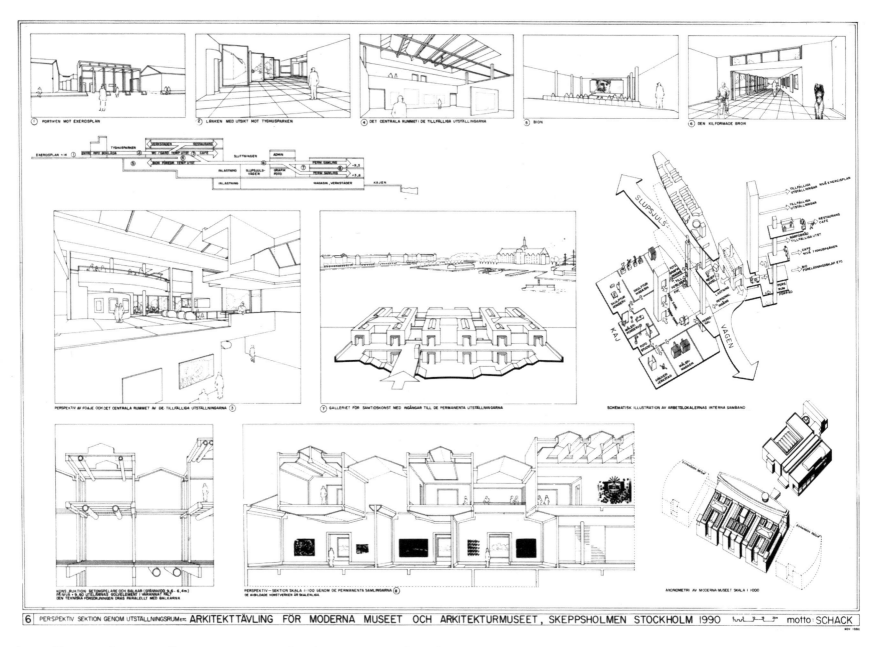

ALEXIS PONTVIK ARKITEKT: Competition entry for the Museum of Modern Art in Stockholm, Sweden. Drawn by Alexis Pontvik Arkitekt. *Technical pen on polyester film.* [*Courtesy Alexis Pontvik Arkitekt (Sweden).*]

YI GANG PENG: Crane Mountain Scenic Area Facilities renovation scheme, China. *Technical pen on vellum.* [*Courtesy Yi Gang Peng (China).*]

ABOUT THE AUTHOR

John S. M. Chen is currently an associate professor
teaching graphics in the School of Architecture and
Planning at Howard University, Washington, D.C. He
received a Master of Architecture degree from the
University of California at Berkeley and a Diploma of
Architecture from Tianjin University in China.
He is a registered architect and holds memberships in
the American Institute of Architects, the American
Society of Architectural Perspectivists, and the Design
Communicators Association. Mr. Chen has conducted
an active practice for about thirty years, serving as
senior designer for commercial, institutional,
transportational, residential, and other projects. He
also provides services for architectural illustrations.